MINI

A DOZEN A ! SONGBOOK

Pop Hits

Including music from Miley Cyrus, The Bee Gees
Taylor Swift, Simon & Garfunkel plus many more...

Exclusive Distributors:
Music Sales Limited
Newmarket Road, Bury St Edmunds, Suffolk IP33 3YB, UK.
Music Sales Pty Limited
Units 3-4, 17 Willfox Street, Condell Park, NSW 2200, Australia.

Order No. WMR101211
ISBN: 978-1-78038-907-3

Arrangements, engravings and audio supplied by Camden Music Services.
CD audio arranged, programmed and mixed by Jeremy Birchall and Christopher Hussey.
Edited by Sam Lung.
CD recorded, mixed and mastered by Jonas Persson.

Printed in the EU.

Your Guarantee of Quality

As publishers, we strive to produce every book to the highest commercial standards.
This book has been carefully designed to minimise awkward page turns and to make
playing from it a real pleasure. Particular care has been given to specifying acid-free,
neutral-sized paper made from pulps which have not been elemental chlorine bleached.
This pulp is from farmed sustainable forests and was produced with special regard for
the environment. Throughout, the printing and binding have been planned to ensure a
sturdy, attractive publication which should give years of enjoyment. If your copy fails to
meet our high standards, please inform us and we will gladly replace it.

www.musicsales.com

THE WILLIS MUSIC COMPANY

This collection of well-known pop pieces can be used on its own or as supplementary material to the iconic *A Dozen A Day* techniques series by Edna Mae Burnam. The pieces have been arranged to progress gradually, applying concepts and patterns from Burnam's technical exercises whenever possible. Teacher accompaniments and suggested guidelines for use with the original series are also provided.

These arrangements are excellent supplements for any method and may also be used for sight-reading practice for more advanced students.

The difficulty titles of certain editions of the *A Dozen A Day* books may vary internationally. This repertoire book corresponds to the first difficulty level.

Contents

Lean On Me

Use with A Dozen A Day Mini Book, after Group I (page 8)

TRACKS
1–2

Words & Music by Bill Withers
Arranged by Christopher Hussey

Soulfully

Accompaniment (student plays one octave higher than written)

Soulfully

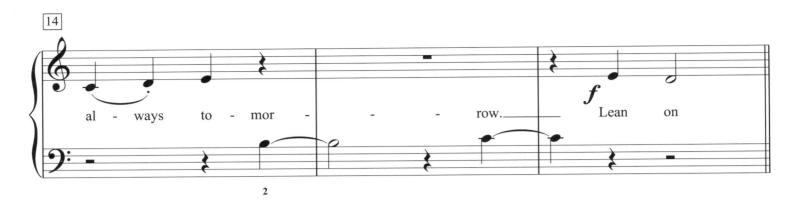

al - ways to - mor - - - row.____ Lean on

me when you're not strong,____ and I'll be your friend,____

____ I'll help you car - - ry on;____

for it won't be long_____ 'til I'm gon - na need_____

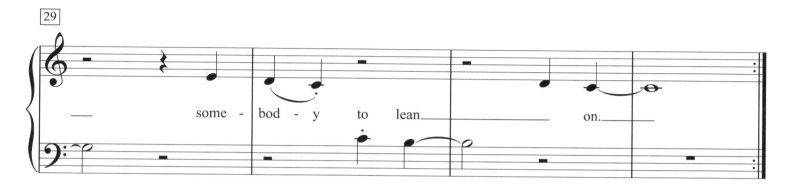

_____ some - bod - y to lean_____ on._____

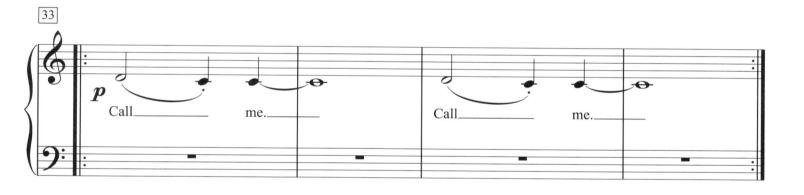

p Call_____ me._____ Call_____ me._____

p

Every Breath You Take

Use after Group I (page 8)

Words & Music by Sting
Arranged by Christopher Hussey

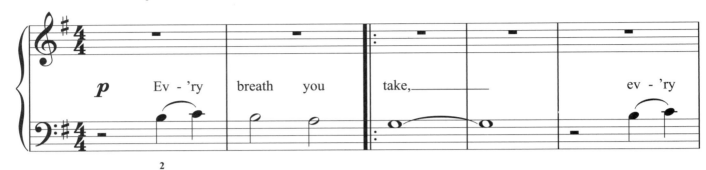

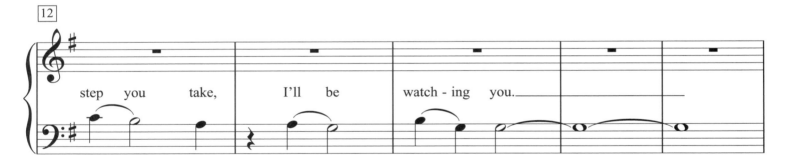

Accompaniment (student plays one octave higher than written)

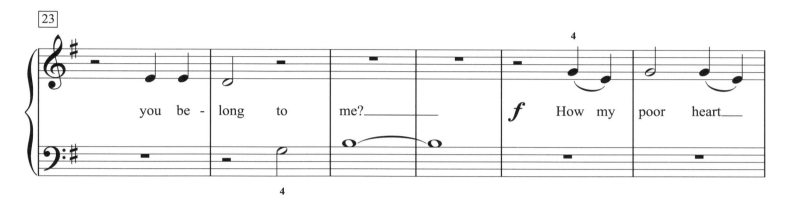

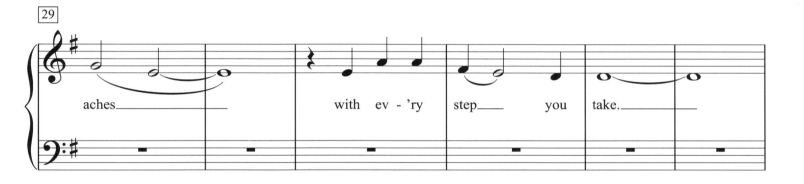

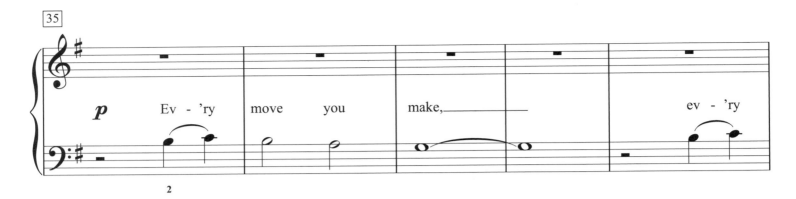

p Ev - 'ry move you make,_____ ev - 'ry

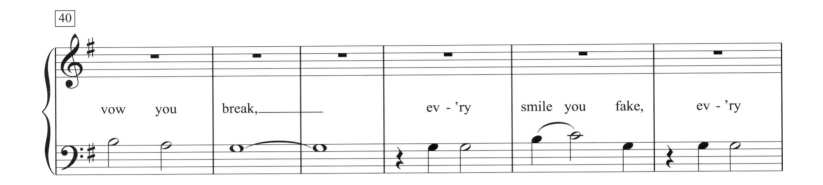

vow you break,_____ ev - 'ry smile you fake, ev - 'ry

claim you stake, I'll be watch - ing you._____

The Sound Of Silence

Use after Group II (page 12)

Words & Music by Paul Simon
Arranged by Christopher Hussey

Sweetly

Hel - lo dark - ness, my old

2nd time: mf

friend;_____ I've come to talk with you a - gain,_____

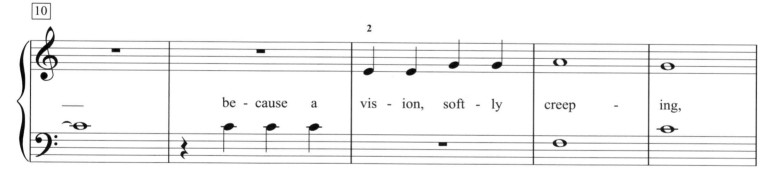

be - cause a vis - ion, soft - ly creep - ing,

Accompaniment (student plays one octave higher than written)

Sweetly

2nd time: mf

10

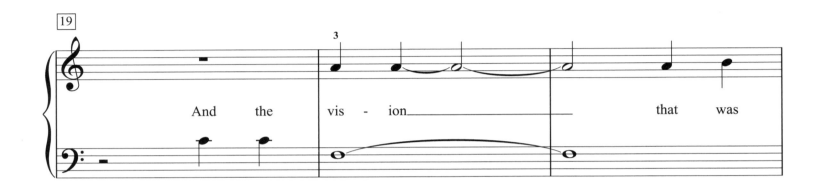

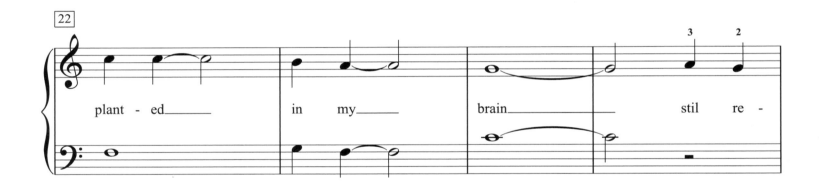

Love Story

Use after Group II (page 12)

Words & Music by Taylor Swift
Arranged by Christopher Hussey

TRACKS
7–8

Passionately

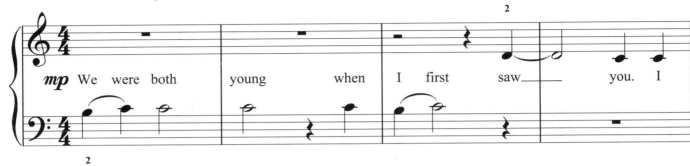

mp We were both young when I first saw you. I

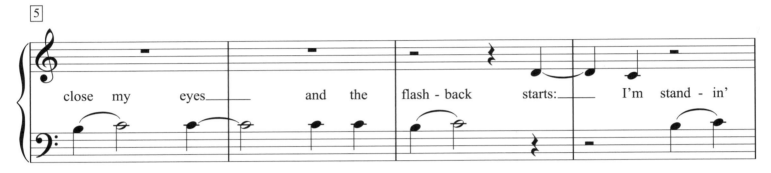

close my eyes and the flash - back starts: I'm stand - in'

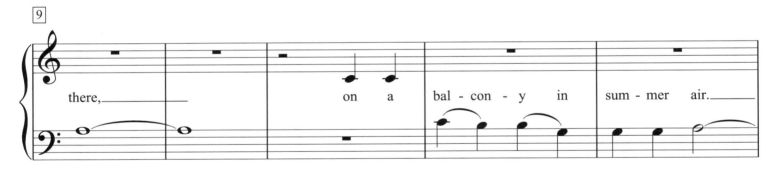

there, on a bal - con - y in sum - mer air.

Accompaniment (student plays one octave higher than written)

Passionately

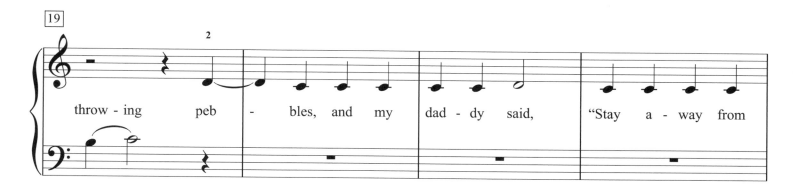

beg - gin' you, "Please_____ don't go."_____

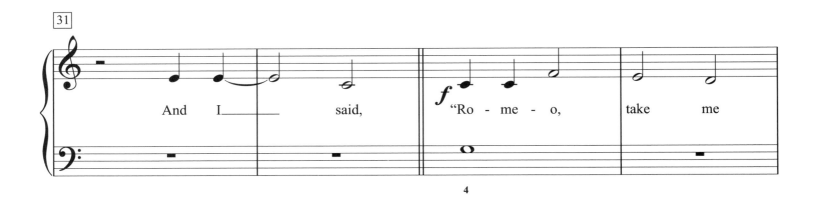

And I_____ said, "Ro - me - o, take me

4

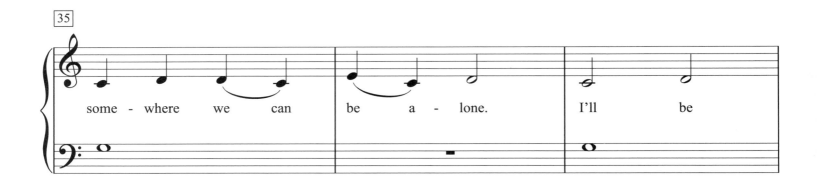

some - where we can be a - lone. I'll be

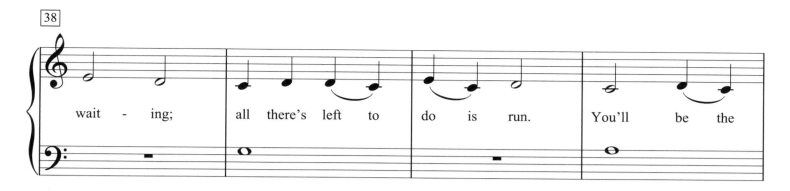

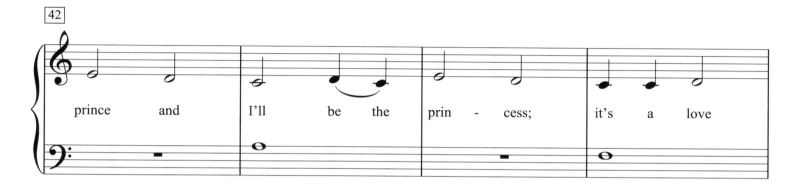

Ebony And Ivory

Use after Group III (page 16)

TRACKS
9–10

Words & Music by Paul McCartney
Arranged by Christopher Hussey

Rhythmically and lightly

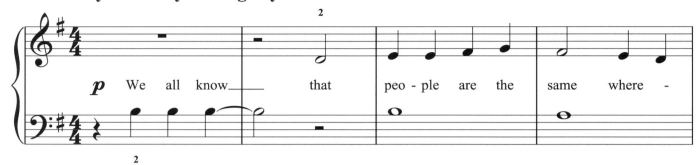

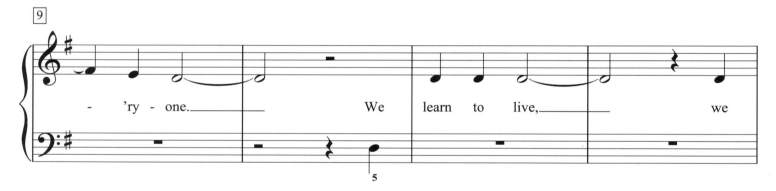

Accompaniment (student plays one octave higher than written)

Rhythmically and lightly

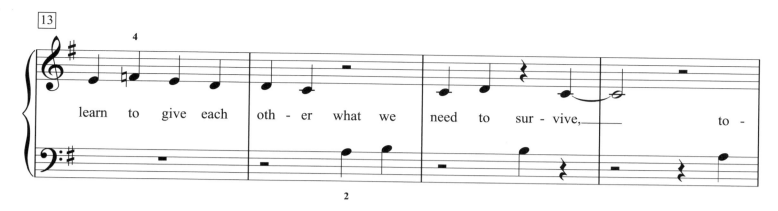

18

Hallelujah

Use after Group III (page 16)

TRACKS 11–12

Words & Music by Leonard Cohen
Arranged by Christopher Hussey

Expressively

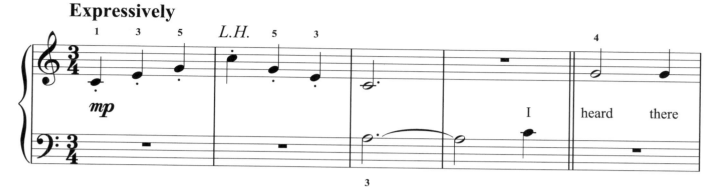

I heard there

was a se - cret chord____ that Da - vid played and it pleased the

Lord, but you don't____ real - ly care for mu - sic, do

Accompaniment (student plays one octave higher than written)

Expressively

ya?_____ Well, it goes like this, the fourth, the

fifth, the mi - nor fall____ and the ma - jor lift,____ *mf* the baf - fled

king com - po - sing 'Hal - le - lu - jah.'_____ *p* Hal - le -

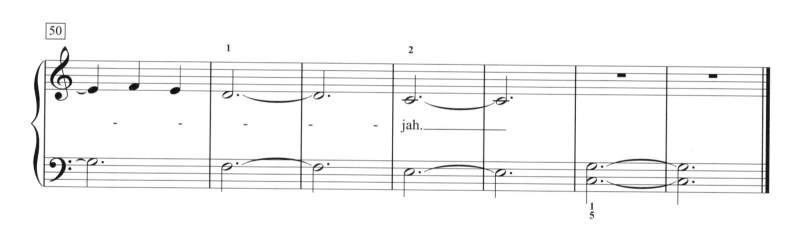

Mad World

Use after Group IV (page 20)

TRACKS 13–14

Words & Music by Roland Orzabal
Arranged by Christopher Hussey

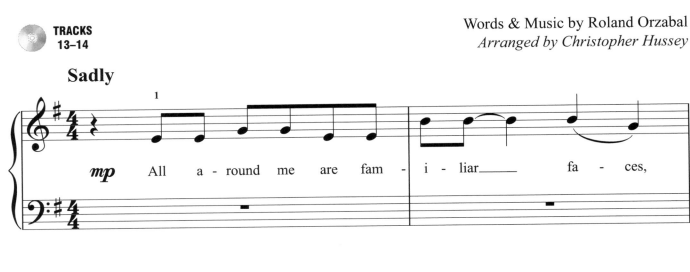

Accompaniment (student plays one octave higher than written)

My Heart Will Go On

Love Theme from TITANIC

Use after Group IV (page 20)

TRACKS
15–16

Words by Will Jennings
Music by James Horner
Arranged by Christopher Hussey

Tenderly

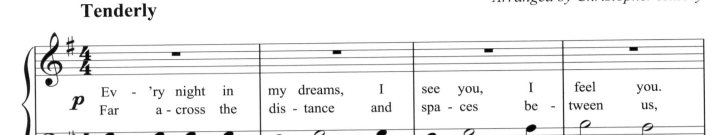

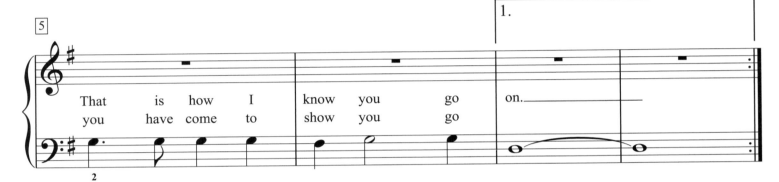

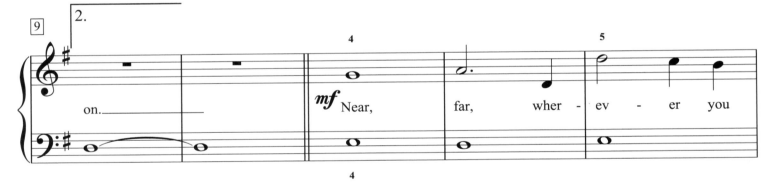

Accompaniment (student plays one octave higher than written)

Tenderly

are, I be - lieve that the heart does go on._____

_____ Once more, you o - pen the door, and you're

here in my heart, and my heart will go on and on.

How Deep Is Your Love

Use after Group V (page 24)

TRACKS
17–18

Words & Music by Barry Gibb, Maurice Gibb & Robin Gibb
Arranged by Christopher Hussey

With a bounce

Accompaniment (student plays one octave higher than written)

With a bounce

© Copyright 1977 Crompton Songs/Gibb Brothers Music.
Warner/Chappell Music Limited/Universal Music Publishing MGB Limited.
All Rights Reserved. International Copyright Secured.

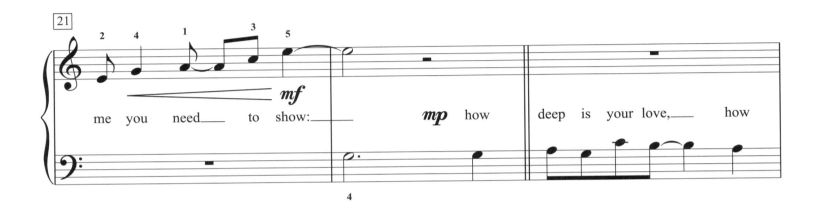

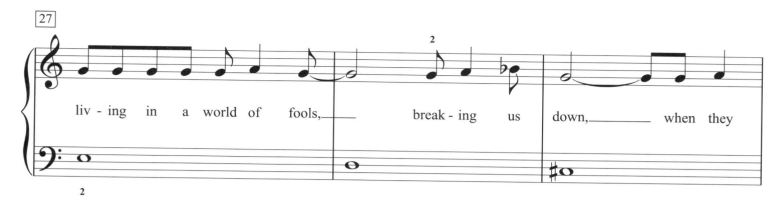

liv - ing in a world of fools,____ break - ing us down,_____ when they

all should let us be._____ We be - long to you____ and

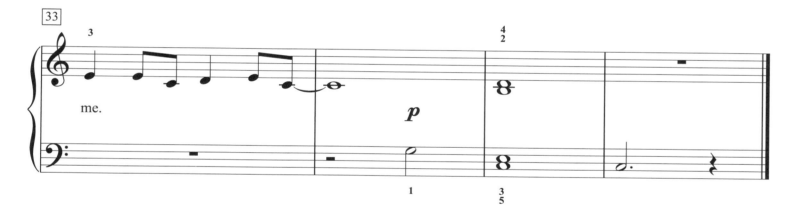

me. p

The Climb

Use after Group V (page 24)

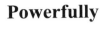
TRACKS 19–20

Words & Music by Jessica Alexander & Jon Mabe
Arranged by Christopher Hussey

Powerfully

mp I can al - most see it, that dream I'm dream - ing, but

there's a voice in - side my head say - in', "You'll nev - er reach it."

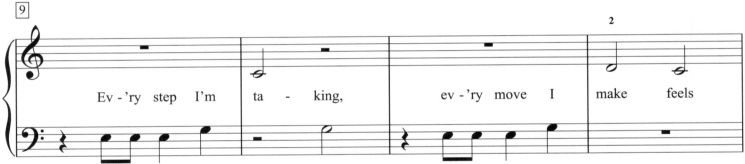

Ev - 'ry step I'm ta - king, ev - 'ry move I make feels

Accompaniment (student plays one octave higher than written)

Powerfully

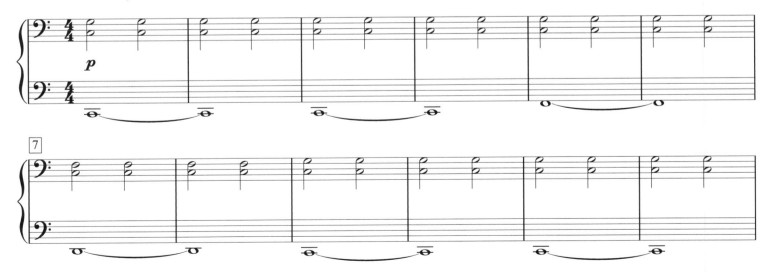

32

123456789